The Answers That Lie Within

ALEXANDRA OAKES

authorHOUSE

AuthorHouse™ UK
1663 Liberty Drive
Bloomington, IN 47403 USA
www.authorhouse.co.uk
Phone: 0800.197.4150

© 2016 Alex Oakes. All rights reserved.

No part of this book may be reproduced, stored in a retrieval system, or transmitted by any means without the written permission of the author.

Published by AuthorHouse 07/29/2016

ISBN: 978-1-5246-6112-0 (sc)
ISBN: 978-1-5246-6113-7 (e)

Print information available on the last page.

Any people depicted in stock imagery provided by Thinkstock are models, and such images are being used for illustrative purposes only.
Certain stock imagery © Thinkstock.

This book is printed on acid-free paper.

Because of the dynamic nature of the Internet, any web addresses or links contained in this book may have changed since publication and may no longer be valid. The views expressed in this work are solely those of the author and do not necessarily reflect the views of the publisher, and the publisher hereby disclaims any responsibility for them.

We are born into the world as pure beings of light, the essence of true love and kindness. To begin our sense of self is developed during childhood, we are greatly influenced by the attachments we make and of the world that we live in. Thus developing our core beliefs.

As we travel along our path we are influenced and inspired by friends, teachers, colleagues and those we love as partners. Our belief of who we are and others around us mirror and reinforce this sense of self.

But as we develop with these beliefs do we lose the sense of who we really are? The true self that was brought into the world, the spiritual being at our core.

To once again attune to the true self allows us to become aware of the internal connections made between past events and expectations of the future. These experiences create the meaning and structure in the 'here and now' and are founded on and grounded in the 'there and then'. The ego is associated with the mind and the sense of time which compulsively thinks in order to be assured of its future existence, rather than knowing its self in the moment of presence.

We all have choice and the ability to create new options should these rules by which we live no longer serve us. Our restricted sense of self can be set free by the power of awareness and compassion. For without awareness there would be no perception, no thoughts. By finding peace and listening to who you are at the deepest level you will find the answers that lie within…

Do you feel like a ship without a rudder, lost at sea with no guidance or understanding of how you got there? If so, then you would need a compass, a set of sails and a good wind to take you in the right direction. Similarly, 'The Answers that Lie Within' will help navigate you along your path. Lying within the pages of this book are fifty-seven abstracts of inspired philosophy to enlighten and guide you.

You may read 'The Answers that Lie within' from front cover to back cover or you may ask for guidance from the Angels to draw you to a page for guidance. Be organic and follow your heart and read these however you feel in the moment.

> In Love and Gratitude,
> Alexandra x

As the clouds open, see the blue sky that lies beneath

And as you look, see the sun and the rays that shine onto the flower below

Without the sun, the flower would not grow

Its bud would be shut.

The flower now has beautiful bright petals that vibrate with energy

They throw scent into the air,

When the world seems dark look for that light and see that although darkness has caused a shadow upon you,

that once the light returns you may bathe and allow yourself to grow,

knowing that without it your bud would not have opened and that this new life would not have grown.

For without the soil the flower would not have been planted,

Without the rain, it would not have been nurtured.

Allow the clouds to pass and reveal the wholeness of the moon,

For within its light receive the solitude & the unity within your soul,

The divine love & the essence of spirit shine to enlighten & lift you,

Allow your worries to float out to the universe & breathe in the peace that shines within.

As you focus towards the subtle petals of the lily,

See the energy that flows dispelling its beautiful fragrance,

For its beauty is natural and as the rain falls it will flourish and grow,

The golden rays of the sun will give warmth and vibration,

Allowing the petals to open and receive the beauty of nature.

Allow the spiritual truths of the soul to unravel,

For they guide you & let you move forward to the wonderful concepts of spiritual life,

As you embrace the love & the awareness of all that is of higher value,

You open to fulfilment & to the essence of peace & true love which resides within the essence of spirit.

Be not afraid my child, for you are a shining light that embraces their divinity enlightening the way for others,

Your essence is sacred and your soul unique,

For you must never absorb the judgements of others that is their path,

Surround yourself with the light and love of spirit & never question the beauty that lies within you.

Allow yourself to fly like the dove on a summer's day,

The breeze supporting its wings allowing it to guide & to take it forward,

Embrace the blue of the sky allowing this healing energy to enlighten & heal your soul,

For on its journey there are many experiences to endure as it trusts that it will find its destination,

The spirit guides & meets it along its rightful path,

Be open & embrace your journey ahead,

For all is part of the divine plan to fulfil & enlighten the soul in this lifetime.

Allow yourself to enter a journey of the self

The universal being that resides within your core

Empower yourself to walk the path on which your spirit calls

For there are higher planes to explore as you recognise of who you are at the deepest level

Embrace the universal energy that beckons you to be at one & discover your higher purpose.

As you look into the light see an opening,

Go forth and do not be afraid,

The light is love and, where there is love there is freedom,

Look forward to the future and as you enter the light look back to the path you once walked,

Throw the light back with forgiveness and compassion,

There is a long path ahead filled with rays of sunshine that filter into your heart as you travel,

You will filter this light onto others to help them see their way forward,

Heal and be healed, you are a light worker.

As you enter the temple of the light allow the transcending energy to fill your whole being,

For the silence encompasses you as you open the window & allow all your troubles from the physical world to float away,

Once you transcend into the vibration of the light, meet with those who guide you, those who nurture you and those who fill your heart with unconditional love and blessings,

Bathe in the energy to allow the wisdom and knowledge to come forth,

Enlightening you and lifting you to a higher dimension.

As you look towards the stars feel their vibration,

Absorb the energy of each one that shines a light in the moonlit sky,

For each one radiates a pure divine light,

As their vibration of mother earth now lifts, their energy helps to lift your soul to higher places.

As you open your heart and are open to receiving great love,

Always remember who you are,

Your intuition is your inner guidance,

So always honour and respect this,

Your right is sacred and your feelings, precious,

As you travel through your journey,

Remember that love comes from within,

You are your greatest friend.

Allow love to take its course, like a dove opening its wings to fly & be guided towards its destiny.

Do not allow any man to question or distort the true feelings of the heart.

For true love prevails & it is not conditioned.

Be Still in the presence of spirit,

Be playful and throw your light in your physical world,

For life is for your enjoyment & your experience to master your Self.

Channel the wisdom to facilitate the growth of inspiration & Divine guidance

For within you have the will & determination to overcome obstacles

The moon embraces the energy that radiates your spirit

Find the peace within you as you focus above into the starlit sky

The peace is the stillness which gives the wisdom to its source.

Dear child be at one,

For the troubled mind is one of illusion based upon the experience of the past,

As you free these concepts & open to new ways of being, you may master your true essence,

Bathe within the beauty of the light,

For never fear the true potential that lies within the soul,

It is divine and it is whole.

Deep within the soul lies the voice of expression,

Sometimes this voice is silenced by the actions of others,

Emotions are suppressed that manifest & determine the direction of the self.

Your soul is the source of your being & love enables expression of who you are,

Love & be loved, allow the beauty of your true self to be once more.

Follow the divine guidance & gain perspective & unity,

Along the path of life is negative & positive experience,

These are the lessons that we learn to aid our growth.

The unity of oneself is developed throughout these lessons,

Gain knowledge & wisdom along the way,

Peace & love will nurture with the divine light of the universe.

Focus on the energies which reside around you,

Befriend your guides as they enter into your energy field,

For they bring love & they bring knowledge,

They touch your soul with divine truth & allow you to blend with them in unity.

Focus on the strength & stillness of your being,

The power lies within each of us,

Great knowledge & wisdom comes from the divine,

Find love within yourself & it will open you to give & receive openly with your heart.

The heart is like an English rose, flourishing as it is nurtured.

Healing from the weathered storm,

Watered from the raindrops & growing in the light received.

At the centre of your being love & honour the child

that lies within,

For the child that has suffered great hurt needs healing,

Tender words & divine love give freedom to that which is trapped within the soul,

For the manifestation of these feelings are detrimental to our being,

Through expression of great love, we give direction to travel safely on our journey.

In the world there is a place,

Where harmony and love remain,

Look inside and find the key,

Your beauty is within,

For others you sacrifice your love,

Your heart is like a beautiful rose,

opening in the sun.

Believe in yourself and in your ability,

Be led on your healing path towards your destiny,

For there is great love ahead,

You are blessed, your being is pure,

Have faith in your soul,

For your soul is sacred.

The words of wisdom from within inspire & direct the way forward,

For we focus on the external when we already have the answers within,

Help & direction come from the divine through intuition,

We are governed by emotion,

Emotion fulfils or destroys our journey,

Through emotion we distort our thoughts & fear replaces integrity,

Allow your mind to still & be quiet, to listen & learn from what you feel within,

This is felt through experience & helps us to learn our lessons in order to direct us forward,

If we ignore our feelings, dis-ease will form in the physical body to warn us to listen from within,

Life is precious. Our self is built from experience of the lessons we have along the way,

Our inner guidance is our remedy of life.

Listen in silence and connect to the love and guidance that lies within,

For the outside distorts and disconnects the knowledge that is within your soul,

Hear the messages that the intuition speaks and do not question the way that you are lead,

Always remember that you are a child of God and that the direction in which you are lead are the lessons that are to be learnt along your spiritual path,

The mind portrays a more external reality, one created by man, one that is never ending and always lead away from your source,

The power within any man remains deep within his being,

For we are beings of light and society now lives in preconceived ways of meaning and understanding,

Love is the source and the connection of the true self and of understanding,

Man is forever searching for new meaning and new philosophy but forgets in the search for meaning that it is always there within the soul.

Should you question thyself or lose this connection then reconnect to the soul, for the spirit within guides you back to your reality.

(continued..)

Only then will you learn to walk again and re-discover the true beauty of life.

The beautiful colour that fills the world with beauty and vibrancy,

The sound of the birds singing fulfils the soul.

Once again you are free and can see that which really matters, you see through the eyes of the source and not through the physical visualisation which has been created.

Love prevails from within,

It is not conditioned nor is it cruel,

True love is the natural beauty,

That lies within the heart.

Master the creativity that lies within,

For it shall flow like a beautiful river,

The current adheres to the direction of its natural movement,

As you work within this energy the beauty shall be portrayed & the true expression of the soul shall be encountered.

In the still of the moonlit waters lies a journey of reflection,

For the shimmering reflection of the moon opens up the potential of the ocean beneath.

In quiet contemplation, allow your soul to journey into the unknown,

For it is with this the horizon expands and opens the consciousness to that which lies beyond.

My child be at peace.

You are worthy & give good intent to serve your highest purpose.

For no man is of complete purity,

You have been condemned & you have been tested.

Do not despair as there is a more peaceful road ahead,

For what you give, you shall receive,

You work in the light & are, so, protected,

The storm has been turbulent but ahead calmer conditions lie in your future path,

Do not punish yourself, we provide safety & comfort.

Oh gracious child allow your cares & your worries to be blown away by the wind,

Focus on all that surrounds you & look at the beauty & blessings you carry,

For the pathway that lies ahead is unseen,

Be assured that as you are led it is with divine intention,

Serving your highest purpose at this time.

Open the mind & allow the divine to unfold the love & the reality of the non-physical world,

As you embrace the beauty of the millpond within you, you embrace the silence & still the mind,

For it is here you shall find value, it is here you shall master the true meaning of all existence.

Look for the petals of love that float around you,

For you can feel their energy,

Fill the soul with the love you feel and allow others to feel the energy that the petals disperse,

For love is given and received but allow the love to flow back.

Love is the source and love is the energy of which will lead us through life.

Look at the beauty of the delicate petals, the softness and the beauty. The beauty of

the shape in which it comes. The perfection of its natural form,

Smell the beautiful fragrance it gives, connect to the way it makes you feel, the way it lifts your soul,

Look at the beautiful colour and shades which each individual petal gives and feel your energy connect.

Love is the source and your connection.

In Divine light & energy we are governed by the principle of man,

Autonomy & direction is within each & every one of us.

For some have lost their way & need divine guidance to continue on their pathway.

Connect with body, mind & soul,

For our intuition guides us, our body carries us, the mind & soul direct us to our purpose,

To heal, man must have faith and heal in all elements of mind, body, spirit,

Through all combined we gain unity & wholeness, we make meaning,

Focus on the truth, the meaning of life, the meaning of existence & love,

The answers lie within us all.

Beauty & peace allow calmness & contentment.

Silence enables connection to divine knowledge & guidance,

Still your mind, allow silence to give you the answers that you seek.

The manifestation of the true self allows you to feel & be who you are,

Those who honour your higher purpose love unconditionally,

Giving love & support as you travel forward on your journey,

Be true to yourself & live life honestly to yourself & to those you love.

The beauty within you unfolds like the beautiful lotus flower,

The negative thought form shall wither the petals that stretch up to the sunlight,

Allow this growth to expand & to grow within the presence of spirit,

The vibration & energy gets stronger as you set your mind free to love which lies

within the universe surrounding & caressing you.

There are many paths and many voyages through which we travel.

Always remember we are always in the rightful place at any given time to grow and enlighten the soul within.

Do not fear in the knowledge that all is in divine order every step of the way

Always speak your truth and be true unto yourself.

Through a Sea of Souls shines a light,

Go forth towards the light,

Where two souls merge as one,

Two spirits that were once as one, reunite

They now shine and light the way for their meaning.

Walk forward and be proud,

For you exude the presence of the spirit,

Go forth into the world with understanding that you serve your highest purpose to

give messages to those in need of the love and guidance of the world of spirit,

Keep your faith & believe in yourself,

For your work is for the highest good of all.

Embrace the love & follow your faith in the knowledge that you are unique.

With the guidance of the light, you are carried on the path towards your destiny,

The direction is straight forward, however others may hinder your direction,

At times if you sway from your path, you may redirect the path back to the road on which you travelled, or by choice, find a different path,

This path will give lessons along the way until you return back to the path on which

you are directed forward.

With time a bud will start to grow, its petals open to heaven

Light dispersed upon its petals as they open to the sun

A little water will then nourish & help the seedling to grow

Until it starts to bloom

As your pathway unfolds you are nurtured along the way

Until you realise your potential

New horizons then begin.

Allow the light to raise your vibration,

As you connect with your source let the guidance bring direction and inspiration within,

For all is divine and love will always outshine the darkness.

Always stand in your truth and honour the spirit from within,

For within the heart there is a love so pure allow no boundaries to hinder your ability to shine this out to others and the world around you.

As you ask for the guidance from spirit the answer is always given in enlightenment.

But it is always given in the right space of time.

It is never too late to change the path at any given moment,

For entrapment is only an illusion,

Always be open to receiving.

In the mist of the storm stand in your righteous power.

For we hold you in protection as you learn a new level of understanding within your soul.

This deep love helps you to experience the soul's connectivity and to hold onto your ownership amongst the turmoil.

Stand still and listen to your soul for we bring the understanding to you and allow you to discover what is truly right.

Stand back and let God unfold this in the highest good for all.

Release fear, release any judgements and stand strong in all you believe.

The waters are deep, the waters are strong but in resilience the wave of emotions will wash over you as you see things from a higher perspective and weather the storm.

Listen to the whisper of the waves, the subtle vibration of the ocean, for the complexity of the mind distorts the subtle messages of your soul dear child,

Do not allow fear and disillusionment to hinder your innate potential, for what lies within you is a light far more powerful.

Listen to your soul, for it calls you to let go and heal.

Detoxification is paramount at this time.

For the lower vibration is pulling at your energy field.

Shield yourself and cut away the cords that block your progress.

Remember you are loved and are a precious child of God working for the highest good.

Allow the wisdom of the Divine to flow through your very being.

An interpretation of the mind will try to validate this experience.

Remember that through unconditional love the experience will unfold in

The way in which it is meant.

For expectancy is built on a past experience and is not of the present.

Through awareness of a larger source, an experience may unfold for the highest good.

For remember a judgement is a state of mind often from which a fear protrudes.

Through the vibration of the earth, the energy rises to life and enlightens the planet.

Listen to the whispers of the trees as they whisper the sweet messages of mother earth.

Allow the solitude to encompass you, let it vibrate deep within your soul to harmonise and to heal.

The green that surrounds each and everyone lifts the vibration of the heart chakra to open and to go forth to give divine love to all in need.

The strong trunk that supports you resonates to give the strong foundation of you all and to support your life force as you are tested by those on the earth plane.

Remember to listen to the messages deep within that we give to each and everyone to help you forward on your journey.

In the mist of winter allow yourself to remain grounded like the wise old oak tree,

For the wind blows and the leaves may fall,

In the frost its branches may become stark,

But its roots are the trees strong foundation and its trunk is the life force which shall always remain strong.

Allow the laws of integrity to lead you,

Embrace your humanity & walk forward into the light,

For the light protects you & guides you to serve your highest purpose,

Draw your guides close & ask for their wisdom in times of need,

For the enlightened path unfolds your spiritual truth.

As you follow your path on the open road you may stumble on the odd pot hole,

Or even climb the odd incline but never lose sight of your goal nor lose trust in your sense of direction,

Others may hinder the journey along the way but, you must trust your inner self to stay on your pathway so that the journey may be accomplished.

As you travel never forget to see the beauty, at anytime, that lies around your path.

See the trees with their beautiful green leaves swaying in the breeze, the birds that nest within them.

For this is life and where there is life realise the beauty of living it.

Be still.

Be at one.

Allow the mystery of the spiritual realm unfold.

Enlightening, opening and fulfilling your inner soul.

For within the peace you move beyond the entrapment of your mind.

Be at peace for within it you shall find your inner calling.

Allow faith to be your ally in times of uncertainty. For we work with you for your highest good,

The path ahead shall unfold, allow it to present itself.

Look forward to the light and see the beauty within others.

Open your heart to true unconditional love and see what it brings you.

Leave behind the past and enter into your new world,

Fight life's challenges to enable your soul to seek opportunities that light your way and bring love.

Open your mind to a world of tranquillity,

One in which peace surrounds you and where there is no malice or harm,

Surround yourself with the colours of the rainbow,

As you study the colours, one by one, you see the message and the vibration that they give,

Release your cares and worries and now fill your mind with light and love,

As you rest and feel your body relax, listen to the vibration and honour what you hear,

Your physical body is your source, one that deserves honour and respect.

Through the essence of the soul we find ourselves,

For he who seeks peace and unity will only find this by listening to within,

Man may dictate or try to enforce power for others to follow or inspire,

But the meaning lives within the soul,

Peace comes from the eternal spirit of being.

The source that lies within is infinite,

Creativity is the source of self expression,

Deep within each and every one of us lies an infinite source,

One to guide and express unconditional love to one's self,

Tap into this source to guide you to your higher purpose,

The beauty lies within this expression and soul path,

Allow divine light to guide you along the way,

For love and unity will lead you to integrity.

Those who govern, self govern themselves,

With self love and self worth you travel along your spiritual path towards enlightenment and fulfillment,

Trust and faith encompasses you along the way.

This day come forth and live your life,

Shed a tear and release the pain,

For pain inside is trapped,

The pain will hinder and block that, which is within,

Once the pain is released you shall become strong once more.

Allow the mind to calm like a millpond on a summers morning,

Let the boats of thought set sail as you float in the peace of the waters that lie beneath,

For there are many hidden depths of discovery to unfold,

Allow the energy to take you to the wonderful world of spirit,

Keep the solitude, and the peace shall flow into every part of your being,

The physical lies dormant as the spirit comes forth to open new dimensions to the life which you know on mother earth,

Be still to the concepts of the mind and allow the energy to take you to the unknown.

About the Author

Alexandra is an international psychic–medium offering over twenty years' experience, delivering enlightenment with compassion. She is extremely passionate about her work and operates out of the highest level of integrity. As a qualified and experienced counsellor, her delivery is both sensitive and empathic. She is a naturally gifted psychic always working from the heart, connecting with the spirit world and angelic realms to deliver evidence and messages of love and upliftment. Alexandra strongly believes that her job as a medium is not only to connect with a client's loved ones but to help empower others to connect to their authenticity and reach their full potential within this life time.

"The beginning of my spiritual journey was finding answers to my own questions, it was a journey that lead me into the lives of many people as a medium, a counsellor, a healer and a teacher. My pathway has led me to explore eastern philosophy and techniques, whilst merging these with western spiritualism it has taught me deeper levels of attunement. I strongly believe that I have been lead to this path to be a voice for spirit, a signpost to help others understand their journey whilst delivering messages of enlightenment."

In 2011 Alexandra channelled and published her first book 'The Creational Force 2012' as seen in 'Spirit and Destiny' magazine and 'Chat its Fate'. Today she demonstrates her gift by conducting personal readings all over the world, offering private sittings for those in the U.K and demonstrations of mediumship together with teaching spiritual development.

www.alexandraoakes.co.uk
alexandraoakes70@gmail.com

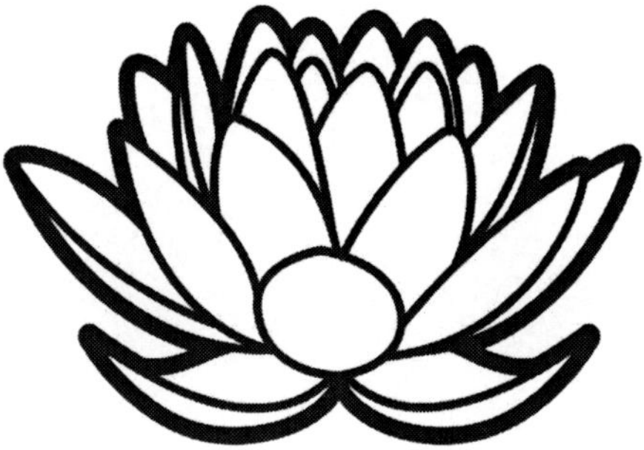